TUDOR CHURCH MUSIC

General Editor John Milsom

SATB

Ave verum Corpus

Edited by John Morehen

Hymn to the Blessed Sacrament, Corpus Christi

WILLIAM BYRD
(1543–1623)

Source: *Gradualia ac cantiones sacrae [liber primus]* (London, 1605; reissued 1610).

Translation: Hail, true Body, born of the Virgin Mary, which truly suffered, sacrificed on the cross for mankind; from whose pierced side came forth both water and blood: be unto us the source of consolation at our last hour. O sweet, O holy, O Jesu, son of Mary, have mercy upon me. Amen.

¹ 'unde' in first and second issues (York Minster, 1605, and Christ Church, Oxford, 1610)

Ave verum Corpus

4

6

Ave verum Corpus

Processed and printed by
Halstan & Co. Ltd., Amersham, Bucks., England

BYRD

Ave verum Corpus

TCM 3 *(revised)*

ISBN 978-0-19-352006-6